## Disclaimer

I0486704

Although the author has made every effort to ensure that the information in this book was correct at press time, the author does not assume and hereby disclaim any liability to any party for any loss, damage, or disruption caused by errors or omissions, whether such errors or omissions result from negligence, accident, or any other cause. The results of the author are not typical.

# Table of Contents

# Introduction

Thank you for taking the time out of your day and for pulling yourself away from your business to hear what I have to say about selling on Amazon. This book will provide a fantastic return on the investment of time you put into reading it, I promise you that. Let me start by explaining why you should read this at all.

I began selling on Amazon in August of 2012. I started with nothing and have now grown my business to about $500,000 in sellable items. I began by taking items from around my house, selling them, making a profit, and then reinvesting that money back into my business.

I had heard of a sourcing tool called Scanpower and once I had enough capital, I signed up. This was one of the best things I have done with my business and I cannot stress enough how essential Scanpower is to the speed we are able to list and ship inventory.

With this new tool and an ever growing understanding of the ins and outs of selling on Amazon, I continued to sell, reinvest and repeat. The results were shocking and grew exponentially as I gained experience and capital In the 2012 I sold $34,000. In 2013 $130,000, then $210,000 in 2014. By the end of June of 2015 I had already surpassed 2014's sales with $260000.

Now, don't get me wrong. Selling on Amazon is by no means a "get rich quick" scheme. It is hard work, but can be mastered by anyone willng to spend the time and take a few risks. You get out of it what you put into it and there is a ton of trial and error. As John Carmack once said, "Focused, hard work is the real key to success. You're your eyes on the goal, and just keep taking the next step towards completing it. If you aren't sure which way to do something," then buy Shawn's book... I'm just kidding, he finishes by saying that, "If you aren't sure which way to do something, do it both ways and see which works better." You can apply this to every aspect of selling and growing.

> # "If you aren't sure which way to do something, do it both ways and see which works better."
>
> –John Carmack

Please understand as you read this book, this is what has worked for me. I have helped a large number of people grow their business, but not all of these strategies may work for you. They are not a guaranteed way to become rich quick, however if you take what I say and apply it to your own strategies the possibilities are endless and I've seen that proven first-hand.

When I first began selling, I started with things around my house. I then began going to stores and buying product, which definitely helped get me to where I am today, but was only the next step. I have now grown and focused a large part of my business on liquidation, which is what we will focus on in this book. It has made a huge impact on the growth of my business (as well as those who've followed in my guided path) and is, I believe, the best way to purchase and sell with high volume profit.

Warning: Your house may end up looking like this after you finish reading!

# What is a Liquidation Store?

To sum it up, a liquidation store aims to get rid of large amounts of inventory that they have on hand. This can be for a number of different reasons such as:

☐ The items are discontinued

☐ The items are out of season or going out of season

☐ The items are nearing expiration

☐ They simply need to clear shelf space for new product

These items are frequently sold in large quantities. This makes for a great opportunity on our end to buy in bulk rather than 3-4 items here and there.

**Warning:** Many times grocery products are expired or are far to close to expiration to sell. This is always something you have to keep an eye out for. Currently amazon will not accept items within 90 days from expiring and will remove them from active inventory at 50 days.

# What Does NOT Work

## Limiting Yourself to Only a Few Categories

Although, before I get into my strategies on what has worked, I want to address the biggest, most common trend I have seen on what does NOT work. I ask people in my groups all of the time what issues they are facing and how I can help them make their first million. I find that most of the time the issue boils down to the fact that people are restricting themselves in what they are buying. Sure everyone has a preferred type of product they sell, but I cannot stress enough that you should get approved in EVERY category possible. Even if you do not think you will sell in that category just get approved. The more categories you are approved in the more you can sell and if you need help, in our groups we network with some of the top experts in ungating.

## Limiting to Clearance Items Only

I frequently see new sellers limit themselves to clearance items only. Sure you can find a great item here and there that is a great seller, but this model doesn't work for large scale growth. This limits you to how much product you are looking at as well and how much time is spent bouncing from store to store. Think about it, where are the clearance items and how much space do they take up in the stores? Not a lot! There are certainly items in a store that are not on clearance that can still make a killing. I am not saying I have never done this. It's a great way to start and if you find a great product why not sell it? However, do not limit yourselves to only the clearance items. We buy TONS of retail at price value and make great profits. It just takes you taking the time to go through and scan every item on the shelf.

I scan everything and if you don't know what to look for then pick an aisle, pick a section and start at the top and work your way down row by row to the bottom. It may take you hours to do, but at the end of your day, you will find many, many more items than you would have just by picking or guessing at items at random. When you do find that fast selling product, hunt it down in every store in your area and buy all that they have. My preference has obviously been grocery, but that's not to say there aren't great buys in all of the other categories. However, groceries, in my experience are easily replenishable, easy to find, and this year alone, groceries account for about 40-50% of our sales. Many people may not think it, but we have had great success reselling commodity items such as sauces, spices, and baking goods. I once found baking soda, again a simple commodity and it was NOT on clearance, at the purchase cost of .60. I turned around and sold them for $7-8 each.

There are always items you may not think are profitable, but even the everyday essentials can grow your business. Regional products are also great sellers. There aren't Wal-Mart's, Meijer, or Publix around every corner so take advantage of that. Items that people cannot buy because they aren't sold in their area or because they don't even have those stores near them can make you a lot of money. Also, try looking up products that are made and manufactured only in your area. People will pay a lot of money for a brand they are loyal to, and you not only have the advantage of buying direct, but also have the ability to pick up the products yourself. Other great products to look for can be items that are being discontinued. These can consist of limited edition, seasonal and baby products (people are VERY loyal to brands that they give to their children), gluten free products, soy products, sugar free, certain flavors, scents, and so on.

## Buying Only What You Would Want to Buy for Yourself

Remember that just because you do not like or would never use a product, it does not mean that no one will. You are buying to sell not use. This is often something that happens subconsciously so do your best to become aware of what you are sourcing and why.

## Buying Blindly

I do not, however, suggest buying blindly. Many times liquidators and wholesalers will offer pallets for cheap purchase, but you have no idea what is in them. I highly suggest against that, as most of the items you will not be able to sell on amazon as new. If you are a merchant seller, do flea markets, or do a lot of junk dump selling on eBay, it may be something for you to consider, but it is very time consuming and you never know what you are going to get. I personally do not think it's worth it. I buy only things I can actually touch, see, and have my hands on. I do not buy anything that I don't at least double my money on after all fees and shipping.

I get asked often if I then buy pallets at all. My answer is yes as long as I know what it is. I once bought 7 pallets of cookies that I paid less than $1,000 for (about .30 cents per item) and turned around selling them for $10 each. If you find the right product pallet buying can be a tremendous option for you. If you do not have the means of transporting them, most liquidation stores have trucks going in and out each day and will deliver them right to you.

Pallet buying is not the only way to buy from liquidation stores, however. You can go in and purchase products at your leisure. No matter how you buy, always look at expiration dates whether you are buying make up, or groceries, or even things like sunscreen. You may have to spend the day looking through the junk for good product, but they have an amazing selection and you can make a lot of money.

# Develop Relationships

An important part of purchasing from liquidation or wholesale stores is developing relationships with the management. I have no shame telling them that I sell online and I tell them what I am looking to buy. By building those relationships they now call me when their inventory comes in and I get the first opportunity to buy their best items when they go on sale. There has even been times they have received their product, gone to pick it up, called me knowing there were items I was interested in, and dropped it off directly to me without even having to use their own warehouse space. It was a winning scenario for me and a winning scenario for them as they made an immediate sale.

# Ultimate List of Liquidation Sources

We talked about the juicy stuff, but now let's cover the big kahuna of it all. The biggest question I am asked is WHERE DO YOU FIND THESE STORES?! You asked and we deliver!

In this section we have listed liquidation stores by state. The work is done for you! Nice huh? Now these stores and their location info and contact numbers were current at the time of writing, but they may not be current depending on when you are reading this.

## Alabama

**Alexander City**

Walker's Bent-N-Dent - 16 Main Street

(256) 377-1733

**Andalusia**

Family Discount Foods - 22709 Highway 55

(334) 881-0169

**Anniston**

Boo's Salvage Grocery - 3100 Noble St.,

(256) 235-2008

C & D Salvage Grocery - 5139 Eulaton Road,

(256) 237-0224

Paw Paw's Salvage Grocery - 229 South Wilmer Ave.,

(256) 237-2506

**Ashville**

B&B Quick Service LLC - 8665 HWY 23,

(205) 594-7455

**Clanton**

Darlene's Discount - 727 7th St. South,

(205) 755-0052

**Dodge City**

Dodge City Thrift Center - 501C Al Hwy 69 S,

(256) 287-0909

**Foley**

Checkouts Inc., - 814 S. McKenzie St. (HWY. 59 South), 36535

(251) 943-4433

**Geneva**

C & M Grocery - 301 W. Maple Avenue,

(334) 684-3473

**Luverne**

Bobbies Discount Grocery - 903 West 3rd. St.

(334) 335-2626

**Nauvoo**

County Line Salvage Grocery - 15759 Highway 5,

(205) 697-2400

**Piedmont**

Piedmont Salvage Grocery - 106 East Alabama Street

(256) 447-8602

**Shelby**

Shelby Discount Grocery - 4814 Highway 47,

(205) 670-0038

**Talladega**

Ted's Discount Market - 217 Coosa St East,

(256) 362-5868

**Verbena**

Sandy's Bent-N-Dent Grocery - 6545 US Highway 31,

(205) 755-4301

# Arizona

**Cornville**

Grocery Surplus Outlet LLC., - 9435 Cornville Road,

(928) 639-3869

**Mesa**

American Discount Foods - 308 South Extension Road. 108,

(480) 649-4495

**Parker**Craazy Taazy Discount Store - 820 California Ave,

(928) 669-2548

**Peoria**

The Dented Can LLC, -  9501 W Peoria Ave Ste 11,

(623) 486-9646

**Phoenix**

Grocery Outlet - 4308 W Bell Rd.,

(602) 548-0007

**Quartzsite**

Discount Groceries - 1558 West Main St.,

(928) 927-4301

**San Luis**

Green Tree Grocery Outlet - 520 N. Archibald Street

**Yuma**

D' Real Deal - 2101 W. 8th St.,

(928) 343-1227

Green Tree Grocery Outlet - 495 E. 10th Street,
(928) 329-6664
Green Tree Grocery Outlet - 9117 E. South Frontage Road
(in the Foothills)

# Arkansas

**Alma**
A-Z Distributors, LLC - 4810 N. Hwy 71
(479) 632-1002
**Beebe**
Beebe Discount Food Salvage Grocery -  214 1/2 West Center St.,
(501) 416-5161
**Berryville**
Berryville Discount Groceries - 510 N. Mail St.,
(870) 423-1030
**Bismarck**
Bag-a-Bargain - 12281 Hwy. 84 Ste. 2,
(501) 865-2333
**Dardanelle**
Midway Discount Groceries - 21779 N. Hwy. 27,
(479) 229-3368
**East Salem**
Stiles Discount Grocery - Hwy 62-412,
(870) 895-4800

**Elkins**
White River Discount Foods - 2421 North Center Street,
(479) 251-1425

**Eureka Springs**

W. T. Focker Discount Grocery - 369 CR 207 (Onyx Cave Rd)

**Green Forest**

The Country Rooster, 101 Phillips on the Main Square,
(870) 480-6170

**Harrison, South Harrison**

Harrison's Bent & Dent Grocery - 3864 Highway 7 South,
(870) 391-2210Wholesale Outlet, - 519 North Main Street,
(870) 743-5248

**Huntsville**

Ma & Pa Bent N Dent Groceries - 15045 Highway 412,
(479) 738-6272

**Lincoln**

62 Surplus - 110 W. Pridemore ,
(479) 824-1480

**Midland City**

Discount Groceries - Highway 231 South,
(334) 983-1250

**Mulberry**

Higgen's Produce (and Grocery) - 3741 Mulberry,
(479) 997-8601

**Nophlet**

Z & C Salvage Grocery - 300 W Padgett Street,
(870) 665-9692

**Salem**

Highway 62 (Call for directions)
(870) 895-4800

**Western Grove**

Country Cupboard - Rt. 1 Box 273,

(870) 429-5046

# California

**Angel's Camp**

Food Buys and Beyond - 328 N. Main Street

**Atascadero**

Grocery Discount Center - 7075 El Camino Real,

(805) 460-9341

**Bakersfield**

Manny's Discount Grocery - 522 East 19th Street

(661) 328-0703Grocery Outlet Bargain Mart - 6421 Ming Ave.,

(661) 833-2180

**Berkeley**

Grocery Outlet - 2001 4th Street,

(510) 666-0670

**Bloomington**

Oliver's Discount Grocery - 18829 Valley Blvd.,

(909) 874-0915

**Bodfish**

Manny's Discount Grocery - 3864 Lake Isabelle Blvd.,

(760) 379-3115

**Chico**

Grocery Outlet - 2157 Pillsbury Road,

(530) 345-2666

**Crescent City**

Grocery Outlet - 1124 3rd St.,

(530) 464-3131

**Delano**

California Discount Grocery - 1835 Glenwood St.,

(661) 725-4820

**Granite Bay**

Grocery Outlet - 4080 Douglas Blvd.,

(916) 789-7322

**Hayward**

Grocery Outlet - 22660 Vermont St.,

(510) 881-8020

Grocery Outlet - 426 West Harder Rd.

**Hemet**

Grocery Outlet - 1470 East Florida Ave,

(951) 766-8819

**National City**

Grocery Outlet - 3446 Highland Ave,

(619) 420-7134

**Oakhurst**

Grocery Discount Center - 49333 Road 426 Suite B,

(559) 683-5429

**Oakland**

Grocery Outlet - 2900 Broadway,

(510) 465-5649

**Redwood City**

Grocery Outlet - 1833 Broadway St,

(650) 364-7406

**San Bernardino**

Mike & Judie's Grocery Warehouse - 580 South Inland Ctr. Drive, (909) 885-8381

**Santa Rosa**

Grocery Outlet - 1116 4th St.,

(707) 566-0530

**Tehachapi**

Overstock Foods - 555 West Tehachapi Bl.,

(661) 822-8546

**Tracy**

Grocery Outlet - 825 W. Eleventh,

(209) 836-2182

**Turlock**

Pop's Bargain Outlet - 468 S. Center St.,

(209) 668-7156

**Van Nuys**

15757 Stagg Street,

(818) 849-5195

**Wasco**

2 Broke Discount Grocery - 652 E Street,

(661) 717-9059

**Whittier**

Manuel's Discount - 11917 Washington Blvd.,

(562) 696-1035

# Colorado

**Arvada**

Friday Store - 5636 Newland Way

**Brighton**

Robb's Inc., - 301 S Main St.

**Colorado Springs**

SouthSide BargainMart - 3075 South Academy Boulevard.,

(719) 434-8639

Central Bargain Mart - 3999 Palmer Park,

(719) 597-1498
https://www.facebook.com/ColoradoSpringsBargainMart

Extreme Bargains - 2727 Palmer Park Boulevard,

(719) 448-0757

Extreme Bargains - 3190 N. Stone Avenue,

(719) 471-8506

Extreme Bargains - 3112 East Platte,

(719) 473-6974

The Open Box, LLC Discount Electronics - 2727 Palmer Park,

(719) 448-0759

**Dacono**

Dacona Discount Grocery - 913 Carbondale Drive,

(303) 833-5005

**Fort Lupton**

Robb's Inc., - 511 McKinley Ave,

(303) 857-1459

**Greeley**

12th Street Pantry - 716 12th Street,

(973) 356-7747

**Loveland**

Esh Discount Grocery - 4221 West Eisenhower,
(970) 612-0160

**Monte Vista**

Sunshine Salvage LLC - 10978 S County Rd 5E,
(719) 852-6981

**Pueblo**

Markdown Market - 1216 South Prairie Avenue,
(719) 561-0542

# Connecticut

**Morris**

Sugar Mountain Farm - 310 Watertown Road,
(860) 274-0341

# Delaware

**Dover**

Byler's Country Store - 1368 Rose Valley School Road,
(302) 674-1689

**Harrington**

Blyer's Country Store - 1 Liberty Plaza,
(302) 398-02398

# Florida

**Bonita Springs**

Dixie Liquidation Groceries - 9080 Bonita Beach Road,
(239) 992-1002

**Bradenton**

Petrik Salvage Market - 1721 9th. Street West,
(941) 747-3194

**Crystal River**

Dollars & Dents - 1321 SE US Highway 19,
(352) 795-9495

**Dade City**

Tin Can Pams - 14444 7th St.
(352) 567-3719

**Englewood**

Stretch-A-Dollar Outlet - 2801 Placida Road,
(941) 697-0275

**Floral City**

SaveSmart - 8640 S. Florida Avenue,
(352) 341-1947

**Ft. Myers**

Liquidation Outlet - 3853 Cleveland Av (US HWY 41)
(239) 770-7603

**Freeport**

Bargains & More - 15890 Business 331,
(850) 880-6175

**Groveland**

Groveland Discount Grocery - 141 Howey Rd,
(352) 429-4299

**Holiday**

Webb's 99 Cents Superstore & More - 2607 US Hwy. 19,
(727) 943-5841

**Jacksonville**

C&B Salvage - 3811 West University Blvd., Unit 13,
(904) 725-3477 J&W Discount - 4045 Post St.,
(904) 387-4651 Solomon Ventures - 1650 Art Museum Drive,
(904) 306-9300

**Lake Alfred**

Discount Foods, Inc., - 750 East Alfred St. (Hwy 1792),
(863) 956-5253

**Melbourne**

Discount Dave's Grocery Outlet – 1518 S Babcock Street
(321) 984-1009

**Ocala**

Oma's Gerneral Store of Ocala, LLC., -  2640-A NW 10th Street,
(352) 401-9330
I-75 Super Flea Market - 4121 NW 44th Ave.,
(352) 351-9220

**Orlando**

Sacks Grocery Outlet - 6013 Edgewater Drive,
(407) 447-4497

**Palatka**

50 Cent Discount Grocery - Hwy 17 & Horselanding Road,
(888) 418-7754

**Palmetto**

V J's Grocery Inc., - 737 8th Ave West Suite A
(941) 729-2776

**Pensacola**

Bent and Dent Grocery - 935 N New Warrington Rd,
(850) 393-9500

Discount Goods & Groceries - 935 North New Warrington Rd.,
(850) 393-9500

Lowery's Discount Grocery - 4801 N Palafox,
(850) 607-2360

**Perry**

Foster's - 1305A N. Jefferson St.,
(850) 584-2795

**Ruskin**

Gully's Surplus Grocery - 720 N. US Highway 41,
(813) 645-4801

**Saint Augustine**

Discount Groceries & More - 233 State Road 16,
(904) 827-0660

**Stuart**

L & G Discount Grocery - 2201 SE Indian St,
(772) 287-1404

**Tampa**

D & S Bargain Store & Salvage - 6222 E Columbus Dr,
(813) 621-3811

**Wildwood**

Tin Can Pams - 1006 N Main St.,

(352) 748-4666

**Winter Haven**

Discount Foods, Inc., - 801 Spirit Lake Rd,

(863) 299-6271

# Georgia

**Brooklet**

Discount Foods - 533 US Highway 80 East,

(912) 842-5656

**Buford**

Hill Brothers Grocery & Salvage - 122 E Shadburn Ave,

(770)-945-7218

**Carrollton**

T & W Salvage Grocery - 3947 North Highway 27,

(770) 838-9897

$1 Grocery Store - 3743 Hwy 27 North,

(770) 830-7433

**Cartersville**

B & B Salvage Grocery - 1350 Joe Frank Harris Pkwy SE,

(770) 382-7041

**Cedartown**

Brooks Salvage Grocery - 1028 East Ave.,

(770) 748-4881

**Columbus**

Nick N-Dent, 1167 Henry Avenue,

(706) 576-6840

**Covington**

Bells Discount Groceries - 11377 Brown Bridge Rd.,

(770) 787-8800

**Griffin**

Wilson's Warehouse - 830 E Broadway St,

(770) 229-9154

**Hinesville**

Tin Can Sam's Discount Grocery - 4215 B. West Oglethorpe Hwy.,
(912) 876-7231

**Temple**

Robinson discount Grocery - 321 Sage Street,

(770) 562-1317

**Villa Rica**

Buy Smart - 760 W Bankhead Hwy.,

(770) 459-4102

# Hawaii

**Hilo**

Cost U Less - 715 Kinoole Street,

(808) 933-3031

# Idaho

**Boise**

Grocery Outlet - 5544 West Fairview Avenue,

(208) 376-2953

**Twin Falls**

Grocery Outlet - 2318 Addison Ave East,

(208) 734-0293

# Illinois

**Arcola**

Country Salvage Store - 427 East County Road 200N,

(217) 268-3698

**Carmi**

Little Giant Grocery Outlet - 1347 IL HWY 1

(618) 382-3347

https://www.facebook.com/LittleGiantGroceryOutlet

**Chicago**

Continental Salvage, Inc. DBA Continental Sales "Lots 4 Less," 6333 S. Cicero Ave, 60638

(773) 581-8100

**East Dundee**

Discount Grocery Outlet - 220 Dundee Ave,

(847) 836-8000

**Rapids City**

Can Ladies - 224 13th Street,

(309) 496-1900

**Wayne City**

Greenfield Discount Grocery - RR 2 Box 136

# Indiana

**Bremen**

Pinehill Discount - 1800 5th Rd,

(574) 546-2117

**Butler**

Phil's Discount Grocery - 124 South Broadway,

(260) 868-2400

**Goshen**

The Dented Can - 25743 State Road 119,

(574) 862-2212

**Indianapolis**

Angelo's - 201 S College Ave,

(317) 634-6552

**Jamestown**

Jamestown Discount Variety

(765) 276-4688

**La Fontaine**

Food Cupboard Inc., - 205 Logan Avenue,

(765) 981-4600

## Leesburg

Triple T Outlet salvage discount groceries - 4454 N State Road 13, (574) 834-5442 – Primary  (574) 834-7595

## Ligonier

Four Seasons Deals - 6298 900N Ligonier, IN 46767,

(260) 894-4344

KJ's - 10818 N. 700 W.,

(260) 593-0444

## Macy

Raber's Kountry Store - 14493 N. State Road 19,

(574) 893-4223

## Middlebury

Forks County Line Stores, Inc., - 508 East Warren St.,

(574) 825-5896

## Mishawaka

S & P Discount Grocery - 2100 Lincolnway W, Mishawaka, IN
(574) 255-2997

## Nappanee

Stettas Discount Inc., - 13452 N 950 W,

(574) 773-0508

## New Haven

24/30 Surplus - 218 State Road 930 West,

(260) 493-1951

## North Judson

Bailey's Discount Center - 5900 S. Range Rd,

(574) 896-3889

## Richmond

B&D Grocery Outlet - 440 S 9th St,

(765) 962-8646

**South Bend**

Dents for Cents Discount Grocery - 1905 Goodson Ct.,

(574) 234-DENT

**Shipshewana**

Forks County Line - 7900 W 310 N,

(260) 768-4931

E & S Sales - 1265 N. State Road 5,

(260) 768-4736

**Urbana**

7 Mile Mini Mart - 255 State Road 13,

 (260) 774-3438

**Vevay**

Dutch Discount Grocery - 10390 North SR 56

(812) 427-2594

**Warsaw**

Sherman & Lins Discount Grocery - 1900 East Winona Avenue,

(574) 269-4320

# Iowa

**Cedar Rapids**

Discount Food Outlet - 5429 Center Point Road NE

**Dallas Center**

Centsable Discount Market - 24163 North Ave #1, 50063

(515) 992-307

**Evansdale**

Joker's Surplus Grocery - 3541 Lafayette Rd,

(319) 235-8916

**Hazelton**

150 Discount Store LLC, -  1664 150th St, 50641

**Kalona**

Central Discount Grocery

**Marengo**

Discount Food Outlet - 2273 Highway 6 Trail

**Oelwein**

CountyLine Grocery - 101 Countyline Rd East

**Riceville**

Heartland Discount - 102 W Main

**Sioux City**

Siouxland Bent n Dent - 720 Jackson St.,
(712) 255-5007

**West Union**

Mel's Country Market - 119 E Elm St,
(563) 380-2017

# Kansas

**Kansas City**

Surplus Grocery Outlet - 3116 Troost Ave,
(816) 924-9576

**Newton**

Meridian Grocery - 101 S Meridian Rd,
(316) 283-4374

https://www.facebook.com/MeridianGrocery/info

# Kentucky

**Campbellsville**

Dent & Ding Discount Grocery Store - 1034 South Central Ave.,
(270) 469-5395

**Edmonton**

The Salvage Store - 102 DaRanco Dr.,
(270) 432-4100

**Glasgow**

Pa's Pantry - 306 YMCA Way,
(270) 629-3003

**Irvington**

Joe's Salvage Grocery - RR 2,
(270) 668-1343

Ridgeview Salvage Grocery - 7510 E Highway 60
(270) 536-3503

**Liberty**

Casey County Discount Foods - 1764 KY 910, 42539,
(606) 787-0957

**Louisville**

B & E Salvage Company, Inc., - 4602 Greenwood Road,
(502) 995-3330

B & E Salvage Company, Inc., - 8504 Shepherdsville Road,
(502) 969-0218

B & E Salvage Company, Inc., - 8645 Preston Highway,
(502) 968-6638

Better Bargain Salvage Mart - 7207 Lower Hunters Trace,
(502) 447-9023

M & M Salvage - 4306 Cloverleaf Dr,

(502) 634-9511

**Muldraugh**

Po Boy & Girl Salvage - 118 North Dixie Highway

(502) 942-0602

**Okolona**

B & E Salvage Co - 8504 Shepherdsville Road,

(502) 969-0218

**Owensville**

Bargains Discount Grocery

(270) 691-0033

# Louisiana

**Bogalusa**

The Salvage Store, - 63116 Hwy 10,

(985) 735-9900

**Cottonport**

Abundant Blessings Discount Grocery - 319 Carmen Street,

(318) 876-3333

**Denham Springs**

Bargain Depot - 8035 Vincent Rd,

(225) 667-6715  - Contact Thomas McFadden

**Folsom**

The Salvage Store - 82540 Highway 25,

(985) 796-9114

**Franklinton**

The Salvage Store, - 1914 Washington St.,
 (985) 893-5959

**Jena**

The Old Country Store - 686 Airport Drive,
(318) 880-7939

**Kentwood**

B & D Salvage Grocery - 600 1st Street,
(985) 229-5323

**New Orleans**

Suda Salvage Company - 5821 Jefferson Highway,
(504) 733-3660

**Pearl River**

Hickory Salvage Company - 67736 Highway 41
(985) 863-5498

**Pollock**

Brooks Discount Grocery,
(318) 765-2110

# Maine

**Chelsea**

Bell's Liquidation - Route 17

**Waterville**

Caswell's Discount Wholesale - 68 Armory Road,
(207) 873-5181

# Maryland

**Elkton**

Molly's Bargain Barrel - 555 Blue Ball Road,

(443) 309-4548

**Forest Hill**

121A Industry Lane, Suite 7,

(410) 420-8544

**Oakland**

Stop And Save Foods - 4137 Maryland Highway,

(301) 334-6005

**Preston**

Bill's Salvage Sales - Payne Road,

(410) 673-2619

# Massachusetts

**Boston**

Discount Grocery Store - 3 Columbus Ave. Ste 2,

(866) 945-5346

**Greenfield**

The Barn - 95 River St.,

(413) 774-5599

**Indian Orchards**

Save-A -Lot Food Stores - 459 Main St.,

(413) 543-0200

**Northampton**

Deals & Steals - 7 Pearl Street,

(413) 586-5654

**Springfield**

Price Rite - 633 Boston Road,

(413) 796-2934

Price Rite - 655 Liberty St.,

(413) 732-4405

# Michigan

**Bay City**

Blue Knight Salvage Foods - 3286 South Huron Road,

(989) 686-5540

**Bear Lake**

Bear Lake Discount Grocery - 11740 Chippewa Hwy.,

(231) 864-4640

**Brown City**

Bailey's Variety Store - 4771 Bailey Road, Contact

(989) 761-7714

**DeWitt**

Mor For Less - 16795 S. Business 27,

(517) 372-5096

**Evart**

Wieler's Food Mart - 5938 W US-10,

(231) 734-9730

**Farwell**

Hook 'em Discounts - 199 W. Main,

(989) 588-3200

**Grand Rapids**

Community Grocery Outlet - 1255 Michigan NE,

(616) 558-0868

**Grandville**

M & B Foods - 2900 Wilson Avenue SW #5,

(616) 249-0081

**Hale**

M&M Discount Groceries - 3566 County Line Rd.,

(989) 305-0034

**Haslett**

Sav-A-Lot Food Stores - 16912 Marsh Rd.,

(517) 339-9670

**Homer**

Kryst Farm Market - 8451 Van Wert Rd.

**Hudsonville**

Morrie's Grocery Outlet - 2410 Chicago Dr.

**Lansing**

Sav-A-Lot Food Stores - 3222 S. Martin Luther King Jr. Blvd.,

(517) 394-0396

**McBane**

Pineview Discount Store - 9200 S. Burkett Road,

(231) 825-2892

**Mio**

Country Corners - 1284 W. Kittle Road,

(989) 826-6063

**Newaygo**

Brookside Discount Grocery - 3701 W 72nd St.,
(231) 924-9118

**Otisville**

Denny's Supermarket - 410 N. State Rd.,
(810) 631-6390

**Sand Lake**

Verns Wooden Nickle - 70 2nd Street,
(616) 636-5795

**Scottville**

The Mercantile - 707 W. US 10,
(231) 757-9130

**Sparta**

Andy Discount Grocery - 572 S. State Street,
(616) 887-1999

**Sturgis**

Misfit Foods LLC, - 116 North Centreville Rd

# Minnesota

**Anoka**

Mike's Discount Foods - 516 E River Rd,
(763) 422-8615

**Fridley**

Mike's Discount Foods - 230 Osborne Rd NE,
(763) 572-2254

**Hancock**

Meadowland Market - 583 6th Street,
(320) 392-5050

**Hilltop**

Mike's Discount Foods - 905 45th Ave NE,

(763) 502-8999

**Hutchinson**

A Great Sale - 1060 Hwy 15 S,

(320) 587-0500

**Minneapolis**

So Lo Grocery Outlet - 3111 Emerson Av. N.,

(612) 302-8855

**New London**

Pete's Surplus - Junction Highway 9 & 71

(320) 354-2626

**Rushford**

Litscher's Meat Processing & Discount Grocery - 106 West Park,

(507) 864-7906

**St. Cloud**

Gopher Bargain Center - 229 Lincoln AVE N.E.,

(320) 252-3311

**Waite Park**

Clearance Grocery Center - 506 West Division St.,

(320) 257-8884

# Mississippi

**Batesville**

Wanda's Salvage Grocery - 109 Highway 51 S,

(662) 563-0476

**Booneville**

Discount Grocery - 519 East Church Street,

(662) 728-6409

R & W Salvage Grocery - 2016 East Chambers Dr.,

(662) 728-0099

**Burnsville**

Dollar Wise Discount grocery - 373 Highway 72,
(662) 427-8840

**Brooklet**

Discount Grocery - 533B US Highway 80 East,

(912) 842-5656

**Burnsville**

Dollar Wise Discount grocery - 373 Highway 72,

(662) 427-8840

**Byhalia**

Discount Grocery - 8543 Hwy. 178 W.,

(662) 838-3776

**Collins**

H & P Salvage Grocery - 466 Highway 35,

(601) 765-0009

**Corinth**

Hwy 72-W Discount Grocery - 2905 Highway 72 West,

(662) 665-0052

**Fulton**

L & R Discount Grocery - 706 South Adams Street,

(662) 862-2925

**Golden**

Silver Dollar Store - 75 Red Bay Rd,

(662) 454-3642

**Grenada**

Discount Grocery - 23291 Highway 8 East,

(662) 294-9950

**Hattiesburg**

Hiatt's Discount Grocery - 819 Edwards Street,

(601) 554-8232

E&B Discount Grocery - 5395 Hwy 42,

(601) 544-1009

**Houlka**

Pat's Salvage Grocery - 3207 Highway 15 North,

(662) 568-7734

**Louisville**

Triple A Produce - 101 John C. Stennis Drive,

(662) 773-8677

**Mantachie**

Shop & Save Discount Grocery - 3562 Highway 371 North,

(662) 282-7820

**McComb**

A-1 Grocery Salvage - 509 Pearl River Ave,
(601) 684-0571

**Mize**

Highway 35 Salvage Grocery - 16944 Highway 35

(601) 733-0490

**Moss Point**

Cheap Charley's Surplus Salvage Groceries - 11200 Highway 613,
(228) 474-8995

**Oxford**

Direct Salvage Grocery - 294 County Road 101
(662) 513-0736

**Poplarville**

Poplarville Grocery & Salvage - 229 Highway 11 S,

(601) 795-2801

Super Salvage - 208 North Main Street,

(601) 795-6655

**Petal**

Petal Discount Grocery - 787 S. Main St,

(601) 544-1654

**Purvis**

Purvis Salvage and Grocery - 309 Highway 589,

(601) 794-5544

**Tylertown**

B & B Grocery Salvage - 309 Beulah Ave,

(601) 876-9514

**Tupelo**

Food Bargains - 1136 W. Main Street,

(662) 840-8037

**Vardamann**

Dao's Grocery Salvage - 118 Main Street,

(662) 682-9898

**Verona**

Penny Pinchers Discount Grocery - 5035 Raymond Ave.,
(662) 566-0011

**Vicksburg**

Captain Jack's Bent & Dent - 1901 N Frontage Rd,

(601) 638-7001

Jimmy's Salvage Grocery - Highway 61 South

(601) 634-1040

**Water Valley**

Highway 9 Salvage Grocery - 654 Highway 9 W,

(662) 473-9880

**Waynesboro**

D J's Salvage Grocery - 119 Mississippi Dr.,

(601) 671-0753

**Wiggins**

Super Savers Discount Salvage Store - 734 Magnolia Drive South,
(601) 928-4483

# Missouri

**Ashland**

Chow's Groceries & Goods - 100 East Broadway, 65010

(315) 939-2332

**Ava**

P G's Salvage & Surplus Grocery - 300 North Jefferson,

(417) 683-5654

**Bahr's Discount Food**

2155 Hwy 100 Labadie, MO 63055,

(636) 742-5411

**Birch Tree**

Beavers Salvage Grocery - Highway 60 West,

(573) 292-3664

**Cabool**

Shetler's Discount Grocery - 200 Industrial Park,

(417) 962-2251

**Clark**

Terry's Country Store (and Bulk Foods), - 4646 Audrain Road,
(573) 819-2730

**Dexter**

S&D Grocery Outlet - 210 E. Business 60,
(573) 624-0001

**Fair Grove**

K & M Grocery - 701 Red Top Road,
(417) 759-9024

**Forsyth**

Tim's Discount Outlet - 15521 US HWY 160,
(417) 546-8467

**Grandin**

Second Chance Market - RR 2 Box 142-En,
(573) 593-4542

**Hollister**

Taney County Damaged Freight & Grocery Outlet - 184 Industrial
Park Rd,
 (417) 335-4056

**Houston**

Stilley Discount - 1591D North Highway 63,
(417) 967-0253

**Humansville**

Mill Street Market - 508 W. Mill,
(417) 754-8787

**Jackson**

Lane's Salvage Groceries - 1227 Old Cape Road,
(573) 243-1805

**Jamesport**

Hutch Brothers Outlet - 208 West Auberry Grove,

(660) 684-6324

**Mountain Grove**

The Discount Grocery - 6893 Outer Rd.,

(417) 746-4233

**Nixa**

Christian County Discount Freight & Grocery - 1284 N. Bryan Dr.,
(417) 724-8600

**Oran**

Dent N Save - 23146 US Highway 61,

(573) 262-2345

**Piedmont**

Janet's Salvage Grocery - Junction 34 & 49,

(573) 223-7420

**Poplar Bluff**

B & C Discount - Highway 53,

(573) 785-7112

**Raytown**

Dirty Don's Bargain Center - 9700 East 56th Street,
(816) 358-9614

**Rolla**

I-44 Surplus Discount Grocery, Exit 189, 11101 Old Highway 66,
(573) 364-6006

**Salem**

Carolyn's Discount Grocery - 300 South Main St.,

(573) 729-2946

## Sedalia

65 Discount, Inc., - 5150 S Limit Avenue,

(660) 826-9242

## St. James

J & J Distributors Salvage & Surplus - 138 West Washington Street, (573) 265-6084

## St. Louis

Cherrick Distribution - 4215 Clayton Avenue

(314) 652-3636

Friedman RR Salvage Warehouse - 5149 Mlk Dr,

(314) 367-5464

## Thayer

Lane Salvage Groceries - 105 Holmes Rd,

(417) 264-7997

Martin Salvage Grocery - Nettleton Road (Route 3 Box 3030)

(417) 264-7699

## West Plains

Corner Salvage Grocery - 1026 Saint Louis St.

(417) 255-9188

**Winona**

Ken's Good Stuff Store - 303 Ash St,

(573) 325-4437

# Montana

**Billings**

Mr Thrifty Foods - 201 North 14th Street,

(406) 252-1052

**Thompson Falls**

Grocery Surplus Store - 5460 Highway 200,

(406) 827-6373

# Nebraska

**Hastings**

Food Cupboard - 522 S Elm Ave, 68901,

(402) 834-0861

https://www.facebook.com/hastingsfoodcupboard

# Nevada

**Carson City**

Grocery Outlet - 1831 N Carson St.,

(775) 882-6199

**Reno**

Grocery Outlet - 3800 Kietze Lane,

(775) 826-7688

**Sparks**

Grocery Outlet - 2020 Oddie Blvd.,
(775) 356-7400

# New Hampshire

**Hillsboro**

JD Food - 192 W Main Street

**North Walpole**

Discount Food Warehouse - 115 Church St.
(603) 445-5317

**Westmoreland**

Stan's Discount Groceries - 1017 Route 12
(603) 399-7737

**Winchester**

Eastern Liquidation Sales - 4 Main St.,
(603) 239-7222

# New Jersey

**Paterson**

Giant International Trading Co. Inc, - 91-97 East Railway Avenue,
(973) 977-9272

# New Mexico

**Albuquerque**
Dee's Discount Grocery, 7000 Zuni Rd SE,
(505) 872-2447
**Portales**
Quality Sales - 612 East 2nd Street,
(575) 356-3900

# New York

**Bainbridge**
Pine Ridge Grocery - 4086 State Hwy 406 13733
(607) 967-5926
**Belleville**
Sharp's Bulk Foods - 8220 State Rte 289 13611
(315) 846-5337
**Lyndonville**
Yoder's Country Cupboard - 10847 Waterbury Rd 14098
(585) 765-3354
**New York**
Jack's 99 Cent Store - 101 W 32nd St 10001
(212) 268-9962
Jack's 99 Cent Store - 16 E 40th St 10016
(212) 696-5767
Jack's 99 Cent Store - 45 W 45th St 10036
(212) 354-6888

**Penn Yan** - Oak Hill Farm Bulk Food 3173 Rte 13A 14527

(877) 536-0837

**Penn Yan**

Hillcrest Bulk and Natural Foods - 2901 State Rte 364 14527

(315) 536-0105

**Port Chester**

That Discount Place - 155 Irving Ave

(914) 305-6750

jane@thatdiscountplace.com
https://www.facebook.com/ThatDiscountPlace

**Savannah**

Springlake Market and Fabrics - 4250 Wolcott Spring Lake Rd

(315) 594-8485

**Seneca Falls**

Sauder's Market and Store - 2168 River Rd 13148

(315) 568-2673

**Seneca Falls**

Glenwood Foods - 2905 Rt-318,

(315) 568-2050

**Syracuse**

Buda's Meats & Produce Inc, - 2100 Park St.,

(315) 476-0740

**Syracuse**

Northway Discount Grocery - 212 West Division Street

(315) 422-9979

# North Carolina

**Asheville**

Amazing Savings - 121 Sweeten Creek Road,

(828) 277-0805

**Black Mountain**

Amazing Savings - 3018 US Hwy 70,

(828) 669-8988

**Charlotte**

BargainMax Inc, - 1000 East Sugar Creek Rd.,

(704) 333-0880

**Denver**

Bargain Center Groceries - 3825 North Highway 16,

(704) 489-2262

**Fairview**

Dickies Half Price Foods - 1512 Charlotte Hwy.,

(828) 628-0834

**Fayetteville**

B J's Salvage Grocery - 039 Camden Rd.,

(910) 426-9670

**Forest City**

J'S Salvage & Discount 763 - 763 US Highway 221A,

(828) 248-1173

**Granite Falls**

George's Grocery Salvage - 3846 Mutt Marshall Lane,

(828) 396-4320

Odum's Salvage - 2474 Connelly Springs Road,
(828) 728-6221

**Jacksonville**

Nicks'N Dents - Ste 3080 G Richlands Hwy, 28540

Contact: Charles Padgett (m) 910-389-6132

**Kings Mountain**

Super Discount Grocery - 108 West Gold Street,
(704) 481-0307

**Lexington**

Salvage Grocery - 4180 NC Highway 8,
(336) 357-0402The Bargain Box - 158 Wiley Lane,
(336) 472-1308

**Lumberton**

Extreme Bargains - 301 North Elm,
(910) 739-9515

**Marion**

TJ's Salvage - 8153 US Hwy 221 North,
(828) 756-8027

**Mocksville**

Food Depot - 3137 US Highway 64 E,
(336) 940-4077

**Newton**

Banana Box Grocery - 1901-M Northwest Blvd.,
(828) 464-6449

**Salisbury**

Discount Salvage Foods Of Salisbury - 3115 South Main Street,
(704) 633-3006

**Stanley**

Jeffs Discount Grocery Warehouse - 103 Durham Road,
(704) 263-8207

**Statesville**

Gene's Produce - 1020 W Front St.,

(704) 872-0479

**Thomasville**

Holly Hill Salvage - No 2, 13 Boyles Street,

(336) 476-6462

Bent and Dent Bargain Store - 345 Hasty School Rd.,

(336) 472-1342

**Tyron**

Jon & Jay's Discount Groceries - 1005 South Trade Street,

(828) 859-3005

# Ohio

**Applecreek**

D & S Discount Grocery - 8828 Dover Road,

(330) 698-0137

Country Salvage Bent-n-Dent Groceries - 9420 Kidron Road,  44606

Paws Country Market Grocery - 8828 Dover Road, 44606,

(330) 698-0137.

**Bellefontaine**

Stites Grocery - 3524 County Rd 130,

(937) 593-9223

**Burton**

Shedd Road Salvage - 15067 Shedd Road

J&K Bent 'N Dent Grocery - 14818 Nash Rd, 4402

(440) 384-0457

**Circleville**

Discount Grocery Outlet - 900 South Pickaway Street,

(740) 474-6501

**Dresden**

ComeUNITY Marketplace - 305 Main Street

Burl Lemon – Executive Director (740) 453-1323 x102

Bill Barker – Business Manager (740) 621–656

**Hartville**

214 Market Avenue,

(330) 294-0876

**Kinsman**

Kinsman General - 6416 Kinsman-Nickerson Rd.,

(330) 876-7283

**Lima**

Daly's Discount Groceries - 506 North Main St.,

(419) 225-2907

Stites Grocery - 8100 Harding Hwy,

(419) 225-9710

**Malvern**

7079 Alliance Rd,

(330) 546-5820

**Mesopotamia**

N & R Salvage - 9217 SR 534

**Middlefield**

B & K Salvage - 5515 Kinsman Road (SR 87)

Kurtz Salvage - 16777 Shedd Road

Maple View Salvage - 17440 Nauvoo Road, 44062

Nature's Nook Grocery & Salvage Store - 12960 Bundysburg Rd.,
(440) 272-5079

Southside Salvage - 15740 Newcomb Road

The Surplus Outlet Store - 15240 Shedd Road,
(440) 834-8311

## Minerva

Overholt's Bargain Grocery & Variety - 912 East Lincolnway,
(330) 868-6644

## Montpelier

Two Brother's Market - 129 West Main Street,
(419) 485-4531

## Orwell

Tower Salvage - 4652 SR 322

## Plain City

Dings 'N Dents Grocery Outlet LLC - 228 Gay Street,
(614) 634-6626

## Quaker City

Grammies Goodies - 63710 Batesville Rd.,
(740) 679-3206

## Rome

Dodgeville Food Salvage & Grocery - 1293 Dodgeville Road,
(440) 294-3805

## Saybrook

Around the Back Salvage - 5223 North Ridge West (SR 20)

## Steubenville

The Pantree - 410 Market St.,
(740) 282-5908

**Sugar Creek**

Brookside Surplus - 2949 SR 93,

(330) 852-4528

Sugarcreek Discount Grocery - 124 East Main Street, 44681

(330) 852-2185

**West Farmington**

Bontrager Salvage Grocery - 172 SecondWinesburg/Wilmot Rte 62

Bent-N-Dent Discount Groceries - 1297 SR 62

**Zanesville**
ComeUNITY Marketplace - 135 South 6th Street
Burl Lemon – Executive Director (740) 453-1323 x102
Bill Barker – Business Manager (740) 621–656

# Oklahoma

**Chouteau**

Crossroads Discount - 305 N Chouteau Avenue,

(918) 476-7696

**Claremore**

Steve's Saturday Store - 302 W. Will Rogers Blvd.,

(918) 341-8002

**Grove**

Cheapo Depo - 530 W 3rd Street,

(918) 786-8893

**Muskogee**

Sooner Surplus - 2300 North 32nd Street,

(918) 684-4000

**Tulsa**

Sooner Surplus - 3190 West 21st Street,
(918) 445-0895

Cheapo Depo - 9206 E Admiral Place,
(918) 835-1109

Cheapo Depo - 5616 W Skelly Drive,
(918) 447-0090

**Wagoner**

The Bargain Box - 603 W Cherokee,
(918) 809-1845

**Westville**

62 Surplus - Hwy. 62,
(918) 723-3648

# Oregon

**Albany**

The Grocery Depot - 2206 Santiam Hwy.,
(541) 926-3874

**Junction City**

Grocery Deals - 93484 Hwy 99,
Contact Heidi Miller – (541) 953-9937

**Lebanon**

The Grocery Depot - 1775 S. Main St.,
(541) 258-3442

**Madras**

Miller's Discount Groceries - 873 SW Hwy 97,
(541) 460-3600

**Molalla**

Real Deal Grocery - 803 W Main St

**Ontario**

Bananas - 532 E. Idaho Ave.,

(541) 889-4866

**Myrtle Creek**

Myrtle Creek Goin' Postal - 729 S Main St, 97457

(541) 863 4446 - Contact: Matt Boyd

**Portland**

Everyday Deals - 17310 S.E. Division St,

(503) 762-4970

Kathy's Shop-N-Save - 11614 S. E. Stark St,

(503) 208-2471

# Pennsylvania

**Atlantic**

County Line Salvage and Bulk - 141 County Line Road,

**Bedford**

Little Barn Discount Groceries - 6200 Lincoln Highway,

(814) 623-2603

Stateline Discount Grocery - 436 Bedford Valley Road,

**Belleville**

Sharp Shopper - 4305 East Main Street, 17004

(717) 935-2392

**Bethel**

Horning's Roadside Market - 8316 Lancaster,

(717) 933-9210

**Bessimer**

B&B Variety - 215 W Pennsylvania Ave, 28016

(704) 629-9399

**Blandon**

BRL Grocery Outlet - 1076 Park Rd.,

(610) 926-4444

**Ephrata**

Ebenezer Grocery - 475 North Reading Rd,

(717) 738-1107

Sharp Shopper Grocery Outlet - 1041 Sharp Ave,

(717) 738-4948

**Exton**

Swann's Pantry - 39 Marchwood Rd.,

(610) 594-2147

**Hanover**

Damaged Freight Outlet - 227 High St.,

(717) 633-1500

**Knox**

Sharp Shopper Grocery Outlet - 100 Knox Rd.

(814) 797-1171

**Knoxville**

R & J Discount Grocery - 202 West Main St.,

(814) 326-4200

**Lancaster**

2108 Spring Valley Rd,

(717) 209-7060

**Lebanon**

Sunset Grocery Outlet - 1650 North 7th Street,
(717) 272-4906

**Leola**

Sharp Shopper Grocery Outlet - 340 W Main St.,
(717) 656-2156

**Meyersdale**

Summit Country Market - 408 Cemetary Road,
(814) 634-1735

**Middletown**

Sharp Shopper Grocery Outlet - 1577 West Harrisburg Pike A, 17
(717) 944-6606 - Linden Centre

**Mifflinburg**

Wenger's Grocery Outlet - 8035 Old Turnpike Rd (Rt.45),
(570) 966-5084

**Montgomery**

Surplus Outlet -  5464 U.S. Hwy 15,
(570) 547-1003

**Morgantown**

B.B.'s Grocery Outlet - 6180 Morgantown Road

**Myerstown**

Horning's Roadside Market - 905 S. College,
(717) 866-7193

**Newburg**

B.B.'s Grocery Outlet - 20 Quigley Road.

**Northumberland**

Surplus Outlet - 281 Point Township Dr.,
(570) 473-7102

**Philadelphia**

San Marc Liquidators - 13451 Damar Dr,

(215) 969-6955

**Pittsburgh**

K M L Sales Inc., - 16 Sts,

(412) 261-5542

**Quakertown**

Swann's Pantry - 240 S West End Blvd. Ste 2

(215) 529-0220

**Quarryville**

B.B.'s Grocery Outlet - 581 Camargo Road.

**Red Lion**

D & K Surplus Grocery - 757 Delta Road,

(717) 244-9398

**Schaefferstown**

B.B.'s Grocery Outlet - Route 419 North,

**Spartansburg**

Byler's Salvage Grocery - Canadotha Lake Road,

**Sugar Grove**

Hilltop Discount Food Store - 6365 Miller Hill Rd.,

(814) 757-5433

## South Carolina

**Batesburg**

Discount Grocery Salvage - 445 West Railroad Ave,

(803) 604-1444

**Greenville**

Amazing Savings - 2710 White House Rd.,

(864) 269-5959

**Leesville**

Discount Grocery & Salvage - 445 Railroad Ave,

(803) 604-1444

**Pawleys Island**

Discount Groceries & More - 10225 Ocean Hwy.,

(843) 241-7015

**Pelzer**

Bargain's, Inc (Bargain Foods) - 349 Highway 8 E,

(864) 947-5115

**Rock Hill**

Discount Grocery Safari - 1122 India Hook Road,

(803) 328-1611,

Facebook.com/madnsafari

**Simpsonville**

915L South Main Street,

(864) 962-1060

**York**

Bargain City - 1803 Filbert Hwy.,

(803) 628-6837

# South Dakota

**Belle Fourche**

Robbs Inc., - 1833 5th Avenue,

(605) 892-4309

**Hermosa**

Pop's Grocery Shoppe - 30 North Fergusen Sreet,

(605) 255-5977

**Rapid City**

XS Direct Discounts - 732 Jackson Boulevard,

(605) 343-4086

# Tennessee

**Alcoa**

DRS Grocery Warehouse Outlet - 3490 Northbend Circle,

(865) 681-1229

**Bluff City**

Bluff City Salvage - 4277 Bluff City Hwy.,

(423) 538-7501

**Burlison**

Bent N Dent - 9121 Munford Giltedge Rd

(901) 476-3000

**Chattanooga**

4758 Hwy 58,

(423) 892-5183

**Chuckey**

R & B Salvage Grocery - 211 Bill Gourley Rd,

(423) 257-7708

**Cleveland**

222 Grove Ave,

(423) 476-1615

**Crossville**

106 Woodmere Mall,

(931) 484-5268

**Dayton**

4009 Rhea County Hwy,

(423) 570-9666

**We Care Community Services**

Food Programs - 1273 Dayton Mtn Hwy,

(423) 775-1000 Mobile – (423) 637-9740

**Dercherd**

Bargain Barnes - 2108 Decherd Boulevard,

(931) 962-0227

**Fall Branch**

Building 5 - 18105 Horton Hwy.,

(423) 348-7520

**Gilt Edge**

Bent-N-Dent - 9121 Munford Giltedge Rd,

(901) 476-3000

**Henderson**

Dollar Savers, - 315 South Church Ave, 38340,

(731) 608-8308

**Hohenwald**

Discount Groceries and More - 644 E. Main St.,

**Hollow Rock**

D & D Discount Grocery - 28105 Broad St,

(731) 586-7569

**Huntingdon**

Pj's Salvage Grocery - 9715 Highway 22,
(731) 986-3589

**Johnson City**

Discount Grocery - 601 West Watauga,
(423) 928-9200

Pierces Discount Grocery - 1207 E. Main St.
(423) 926-2250

Pioneer Market Inc, - 624 Old State Route 34,
(423) 753-2020

**Kingsport**

McCoy Salvage Grocery - 2969 N John B Dennis Hwy.,
(423) 288-8411

The Savvy Shopper - 2461 Memorial Blvd,
(423) 765-1151

**Knoxville**

United Grocery Outlet - 6021 Chapman Highway,
(865) 573-8000

**Lebanon**

Bud's Salvage - 320 N. Cumberland Street,
(615) 449-8085

House of Bargains - 300 North Cumberland St.,
(615) 449-3393

**Lexington**

Highway 22 Salvage Grocery - 22915 Highway 22 North,
(731) 968-5242

Warehouse Salvage - 873 West Church Street,
(731) 968-5146

**Lewisburg**

S & D Warehouse Store - 540 Vista Street.
(931) 359-5944

**Limestone**

R & B Salvage Grocery - 10320 East Andrew Johnson Highway
(423) 257-7708

**Lobelville**

Almost Anything – LLC - 489 Leepers Street,
(931) 593-3444

**Manchester**

Faye's Discount Grocery - 101 North Irwin Street,
(931) 728-1920

**Memphis**

Discount Grocery Sales, - 651 Jefferson Avenue,
(901) 523-9515

**Morristown**

C J Salvage - 4890 South Davy Crockett Parkway,
(423) 318-6291

**Parsons**

Brenda's Salvage Grocery - 370 Cooley Avenue,
(731) 847-4363

**Ramer**

Eastview Bent and Dent - 7733 Highway 45 South,
(731) 646-2660

**Rogersville**

United Grocery Outlet - 921 East Main Street,
(423) 921-3878

**Savannah**

Pen E Pinchers - 70 Harbert Dr,

(731) 926-2710

**Sevierville**

Discount Grocery - 564 Winfield Dunn Pkwy.,

(865) 428-6908

**Whitwell**

The Surplus Store - 13620 Highway 28,

(423) 658-9222

**Winchester**

Sonshine Shop - 1045 Dinah Shore Boulevard,

(931) 968-0092

**Yuma**

Highway 22 Salvage Grocery - 22915 Highway 22 N,

(731) 968-5242

## Texas

**Amarillo**

Panhandle Salvage Store - 5811 South Western Street,

(806) 358-3886

**Athens**

Mike's Surplus Sales, Inc, - 210 N Carroll,

(903) 675-2474

**Big Spring**

Bargain Mart - 403 Runnels,

(432) 264-9107

**Channelview**

S & C Surplus - 15703 Market Street,

(281) 860-0055

**Cleburne**

Healthy Savings Discount Grocery - 1206 East Henderson,

(817) 556-0713

**Dallas**

The Grocery Clearance Center - 3107 S. Cockrell Hill Rd (at Kiest Blvd),

(214) 330-3663

**Dayton**

K & D Discount Grocery - 113 Bryan St.,

(936) 258-0032

**Fort Worth**

Town Talk Foods - 121 N Beach St.,

(817) 831-6136

**Grand Prairie**

Topline Warehouse Store - 433 E Church St.

(972) 262-5326

**Hardin**

Country Discount Grocery - Highway 146 at County Road 2010,

(936) 298-9282

**Hemphill**

F&M Salvage Groceries - Fm 83

(409) 787-4130

**Houston**

Capital Sales Damaged Freight Groceries - 5701 Almeda Rd,

(713) 522-0285

Capital Sales Damaged Freight Groceries - 4663 Telephone Rd,
(713) 649-8658

Groceries & More - 8351 Long Point Road,
(713) 365-9030

Houston Discount Sales - 101 Little York Road,
(713) 691-3586

Jimmy Poole Grocery - 11658 Homestead Rd,
(281) 442-0512

**Kountze**

West Discount and Salvage Grocery - 710 South Pine Street,
(409) 246-8541

**Liberty**

Grocery Warehouse - 2206 N Main,
(936) 336-9991

**New Caney**

Grocery Warehouse - 17844 Hwy 59,
(281) 399-9898

**San Antonio**

AAA Salvage - 1111 South Presa St.,
(210) 533-8611

**Thorndale**

L & L Food Salvage & Merchandise - 109 South Main Street,
(512) 898-2960

**Tomball**

Tomball Grocery Liquidators - 28555 Tomball Parkway,
(281) 744-3290

**Whitney**

Frugal's Discount Grocery - 1218 North Brazo St.,

(254) 694-3714

# Utah

**Salt Lake City**

The NPS Store - 1600 & 1601 South Empire Road,

(801) 972-4133

# Vermont

**Bennington**

Boxes & Cans Discount Food - 160 Benmont Avenue,

(802) 440-8122

Pennywise Discount - 261 Benmont Ave,

(802) 379-0807

**Bethel**

Bethel's U-Save Discount Groceries - 356 Pleasant St.,

(802) 234-6330

**Brattleboro**

Dottie's Discount Foods - 77 Flat St.,

(802) 246-0053

**Poultney**

Discount Food Of Poultney - 298 East Main St

(802) 287-9500 - Owners – Russell & Susan Merrill

**Pownal**

Takoda's Discount Variety - 2848 Route 7,

(802) 823-5445

**Rutland**

Vermont Discount Foods - 1 Scale Ave Ste 55,

(802) 747-0238

**White River Junction**

White River Discount Foods - 80 Sykes Ave,

(802) 295-6264

# Virginia

**Glade Spring**

Discount Grocery - 206 Town Square Street,

(276) 429-4460

**Harrisonburg**

Sharp Shopper Grocery Outlet - 2475-A S Main St.,

(540) 434-8848

**Independence**

R&M Bargains - 101 Hilltop Drive,

(276) 773-3142

**Madison Heights**

Anderson's Country Market - 4133 South Amherst Hwy

(434) 528-9393

**Nathalie**

Miller's Country Store - 1200 Hunting Creek Rd,

(434) 349-9425

### Richmond

Salvage Barn Inc - 5240 Hull Street Road,

(804) 231-1187

Fresh To Frozen - 7154 Hull Street

### Sandston

N&W Salvage - 319 W. Williamsburg Road,

(804) 737-0279

### Waynesboro

Sharp Shopper Grocery Outlet - 2800 A West Main St.,

(540) 942-0975

### Winchester

Sharp Shopper Grocery Outlet - 802 Berryville Avenue #1

(540) 450-1566

# Washington

### Bellingham

2331 James St.,

(360) 671-5152

### Chehalis

J J Berry - 2141 Jackson Highway,

(360) 748-1940

### Deer Park

Discount Groceries and More - 124 E. Crawford St.,

(509) 276-2736

### Seattle

Grocery Outlet - 1702 4th Ave S.

**Shelton**
Shop and Hop - 229 S. 1st Street,
(360) 427-1277
**Yakima**
Grocery Outlet - 2109 S 1st Street,
(509) 452-1777

# West Virginia

**Inwood**
Kenson Discount Grocery - 5312 Tabler Station Road,
(717) 262-3098 - Contact - Jason Atherholt
**Petersburg**
Weaver's Market, LLC, - HC 30 Box 27,
(304) 257-4995

# Wisconsin

**Albany**
Detweiler's Bent and Dent - W363 Atkinson Rd.,
(608) 897-2867
**Beaver Dam**
Dent, Bent, & Beyond - Dodge Dr.
**Beloit**
DJ's Bent & Dent Groceries - 2571 Park Ave.,
(608) 313-0545

**Bonduel**

Country Side Bent and Dent - W4977 County Road Be,

(715) 758-6118

**Coon Valley**

DENT BENT & Beyond LLC, - 219 Central Ave.,

(608) 452-3333

**Dalton**

Mast Bent & Dent - Hwy HH

**Footville**

Discount Grocery Plus - 420 Hwy 11

**Gibbsville**

The Gibbsville General Store - N3125 Hwy 32

**Granton**

The Farmer's Pantry - W3024 Starr Road,

(715) 238-7368

**Hilbert**

Corner Cupboard Salvage Groceries - 44 S. 8th Street (State
Highway 57)

**Marshfield**

The Farmer's Pantry - 301 E. 29th Street,

(715) 384-3291

**Medford**

Discount Foods & Tools - Downtown on Hwy. 64 and Main Street,
(715) 748-2794

**Merrill**

Rich's Discount Sales - 1504 W Main St.,

(715) 536-3032

**Markesan**

A&E Bulk Foods and Bent & Dent - W3884 Grand River Rd

**Mauston**

D&J Thrifty Food Mart - 520 Lacrosse St,

(608) 847-4664

**Oxford**

The Harvest Market - W7341 State Hwy 82,

(608) 586-4303

**Platteville**

12 Baskets LLC, - 185 W Irving Pl. (the corner of Irving Pl. and Court St.),

(608) 349-3311

**Reedsburg**

Jams Bent & Dent - 2029 E Main St.,

(608) 524-1354

J.A.M.S 2 Discount Grocery - 2015 East Main St.

(608) 524-6838

**Thorp**

The Farmer's Pantry - 100 W. Stanley St.,

(715) 669-3400

**Wautoma**

Country Discount Grocery - W9483 Highway 21.

(920) 787-5000

Hilltop Grocery - Hwy B

# Wyoming

**Rawlins**

Discount Grocery - 725 East Cedar Street,

(307) 324-5445

# Tools of the Trade

Pretty amazing stuff huh? Take that and go kick some selling butt! Before I finish I just want to touch base on a few other pointers, questions I get asked all of the time. First, what sites do I use to help find what products are truly profitable.

 As I've always stressed, **Scanpower** is amazing and extremely easy to use tool. They have entended a coupon for our followers and readers. Enter MAYO for the coupon code for a full free month trial. It is an all in one tool covering scouting, listing, bulk pricing & reporting.

**Keepa** is a great FREE tool to help you review a products history. It is a key site to see how well your product has sold in the past, what it's highest selling point and trends have been, and so forth.

 I also use **price zombie** as a great reference that covers many sites and is great for price comparison. USE THESE TOOLS! They will assist you in choosing the best products for you empire.

I also often get asked if I do any merchant selling. I have before, but I choose not to. FBA selling is the way to go and it makes selling that much easier. My team and I swear by it.

The right tools make processing this amount of inventory possible

## Best Seller Rank & Standards

Finally, the last big question I will cover is how I set my standards, or in other words, what rank to I use as a standard for each category. I have a general rule of thumb when it comes to ranks, but anymore I go buy the products trends. We do discuss ranks in our groups, however each person will have their own preference on how much they are willing to gamble in the end. Therefore, we always refer to the graphs and trends via CamelCamelCamel.com and our other sights to see what the actual facts of that product have been over a period of time, rather than a rank which can change daily.

## About Suppliers

A question we are asked more often than one would think, is, "what types of items do they carry?" A lot of people honestly don't know what to expect and many are under the impression it is useless garbage. On the contrary, most salvage stores are a lot like regular grocery stores or any other retail/big box store for that matter. They actually get their products from those same stores and carry most of the same brands you are used to seeing. Depending on the liquidator you can find a lot of the same frozen, grocery, beauty, toys, seasonal items, pet toys, and more. They get their products from stores that may be expired, have minor packaging damage, or have outlived their use in the store, but that doesn't always affect the overall all value and usability of those items. At a grocery liquidator, for example, you can get three times the candy at half the price of a mainstream retailer simply because the printer was off an inch during the manufacturing process. Every item in stores have a shelf life, so once it hits that time they pull it, put it in a box, and then send it into distribution to be sent to liquidation. Again, it doesn't mean there is no value in the product, but stores are constantly getting new items to sell and they will get rid of old ones, no matter the reason, to make room on their own shelves for the new items.

You never know what to expect when walking into a liquidation store, but one thing I want to stress is not to get overwhelmed by the size or un-organization. Some are very organized and may be more simple to navigate, however some may not be. You may walk in and see entire pallets or banana boxes full of product, but don't let that deter you. All that means is that there is great opportunity to make money and even though it may take some time or you may have to dig through boxes, it can be well worth it. You may want to start by focusing on the area you're most familiar with. If you're used to selling groceries, start there, if it's personal care you prefer, head that way, etc. There is no reason to get discouraged as they carry the same brands and products you are used to seeing at any other store.

You dirty store you! Shame, shame. I think many people expect to walk into a beautiful, clean, organized store where the walls are lined with gold and start singing when you walk in. Where the smell of roses and daffodils fills your nose as you walk down the aisles and each and every box is perfectly straight and pulled to the front. Appealing right? Well, don't expect that. Some stores may be decently organized, yes, but many are not. Don't be afraid of a little dirt and disorganization this is a place full of opportunity and hidden gems. However, the people who own and operate these stores didn't open them to throw you a red carpet party or to make your life easier. They usually find a building that may or may not be in the greatest of neighborhoods (if that bothers you), had great, cheap rent, and where they can get as much product out the door as possible. Their priority is moving product in and out and making money, not keeping shelves straight. This is really where they differ from retail stores, but honestly, I cannot stress enough not to let that bother you. These are the same products and the same brands as big box retailers they just may not look as pretty on the outside… or inside. But that is okay don't let it stop you.

# Expiration Dates

When sorting through your items always check for expiration dates. A lot of times this is the biggest hurdle when it comes to liquidation, but again, that's not to say there isn't a surplus of items that will be great sellers. Just be prepared to come across this and, per amazon rules and requirements, they will not accept anything at FBA warehouses if it is within 90 days of expiring. As long as they scan it into the warehouse more than 90 days out from expiration, it can be listed and up for sale until 50 days from expiration, but at that point if it has not sold they will either charge you a fee to destroy it or charge you to send it back to you, so that you can get rid of it as you wish. The same thing happens if you send it in and it is within that 90 day mark; they mark it as unfulfillable and will charge you a fee either way. Personally, I always buy items 100 days from expiring, which gives me enough time to scan it in, ship it, and give them the time to process it before hitting that date.

# Open Boxes and Damages

Another important issue to look for in liquidation stores is open boxes, damages, and factory seals. If the packaging is open or the box is damaged you cannot sell it as new. Any kind of grocery, health or beauty has to be sold as new, but toys, video games, electronics, as well as many other categories can be sold as a collectible or in used condition. Don't be afraid to sell used items as they can still be very profitable, but do always be sure that you'll still profit if listing a used/collectible item. If you do find an item worth selling, whether there are a lot on the shelf, a few, or only a few good ones even, always ask management if they have more in the back. When it comes to open packaging carefully check all items and boxes for factory seals. They may just have tape on them so always make sure they're still in tact and if the seals are indeed broken, they too, can no longer be listed as new and you must check the contents to makee all parts and pieces are there. Not only do all items need to be accounted for, but they need to be in factory packaging and not as if someone took it, opened it, and then shoved everything back into the box. Everything should be in its' original bags or packaging otherwise the product, depending on the category, must be listed as either used or collectible, therefore always cross your t's and dot your i's when it comes to selling such items. As for a little, tiny, itty bitty tip, if you need to remove a bar code or price tag from a product use lighter fluid. Take a makeup sponge, wet it with lighter fluid, wipe the sticker/tag, and you can then easily scrape or pry it off. You're welcome!

# Deciding on Product

An equally significant aspect to liquidation strategy is the rank and how high people are willing to go before turning a product away. For me personally, I always look at the rank history before making a final decision on a product. A lot of items in these stores have high ranking numbers, meaning that the number is high which may normally discourage you from purchasing. I cannot stress enough to always check the historical rank and history before coming to a decision. Take into consideration that a product may have been discontinued by the manufacturer and therefore is no longer available for purchase in stores. The rank may have gone up because the item is no longer in abundant supply and only found on secondary sites, however it can sell for great profit if someone is still looking for it knowing it is in short supply. The product may have been a great seller when it was available in retail so using sites like price zombie, keepa, and camelcamelcamel can be essential in finding hidden gems. I don't ever stray away from any item if the statistics are right and can make me money. And again, I never purchase an item that I cannot at least double my money on after all costs, shipping, etc are factored in.


**Pros -** Cheap price volume ease of buying great volume at one time and smaller market that they're going to sell to. ig you build a relationship with them you know they can call you once you build that relationship

**Cons -** A lot more work. You'll be digging through a lot of items, expiration date items will most like; be expired.

# Schedule

In addition to my personal preferences and strategies, I am also asked how often I return to liquidation stores, how far I'm willing to go, how I find them, how much product do I buy, and how much of that product do I ship at once. I will cover all three of these issues here and it is really quite simple.

First of all, I usually return every two weeks as that is when my payment cycle ends. As I've emphasized previously, I continuously reinvest all of my money back into the business and cannot suggest, enough, to do this especially if you are just starting out. So, every two weeks I return when I get paid and I compile a "trip schedule" in order to hit all of my stores. Every time I return I see new product, so even if you don't find something the first time you check into a liquidation store doesn't mean there will not be something to purchase the next time. These stores are constantly receiving new product so each time a customer purchases an item or items off the shelf they move new items into its' place.

Secondly, how far am I willing to go? Not too far, honestly. These stores are constantly opening and closing, so see what you have near you and go from there. Always call and make sure the store is still open before making the trip out.

# How to Find Stores

So, how do I find these stores? Man, another easy one. Right here in this amazing book! No, I'm kidding. There is so much out there and they really aren't as difficult to find as you think. The best way is by word of mouth. Ask. Don't confine yourself to only the list in this book. Talk to people and see if they know of any discount stores in the area that are not a chain and may sell expired items. On top of that, there is always the Internet. Perform a Google search for terms such as salvage, banana box, grocery liquidation, and so forth in your city. Combine those words, mix them up, toss in a city, and you will come up with something. Do the research, call to confirm, and it is as simple as that.

# How Much to Buy

Finally, how much product do I buy and how much of that product do I ship? How much I buy obviously depends on how much they have to sell, but again, if you find something good and buy all that's on the shelf always ask if they have more in back to purchase. My personal qualifications for grocery, for example, are to buy enough before the expiration date or long-term storage fees kick in. In addition to this and to put it very simply, if I buy a product in large quantities or small quantities I ship it the same - all at once. I do not ship a little here and there or hold on to items, etc. I find good product and I ship it. Again, my preference and this works for me. It may or may not work for you, but this is the strategy I have used and believe in and it works for m

# Conclusion

Well, we're just about wrapped up here folks. For those of you who are not familiar with what we do, the following are the ways to contact me.

we have free Facebook groups:

Groceries on FBA Fulfillment by Amazon
https://www.facebook.com/groups/amazon.groceries/

Retail Sourcing Team: Free Bolos
https://www.facebook.com/groups/freebolos/

Groceries on FBA Blog
http://groceriesonfba.com/

Twitter:
@Groceriesonfba

Instagram:
https://www.instagram.com/shawnmayodotcom/

Snapchat:
https://www.snapchat.com/add/shawnmayo

We offer weekly FREE lists of products online OR Daily lists of products to source that you can find at the following link:

http://Gumroad.com/shawnmayo

Again, I cannot guarantee that they will work for you or make you a million dollars next week, but I can tell you that not only have I had a lot of success with this strategy, but so have many that I not only know but have also coached. My goal is to help others become successful and utilize the tools and opportunities that are right in front of us just as I did, so while I cannot make any guarantees I can back up that this can work if you do it right and make it your own.

Grow Your Amazon Business Faster than ever before without having to do any of the extra work! Shawn Mayo broke into the scene coaching thousands of online sellers to build their businesses and meet their financial goals! Now, he has taken his experience and knowledge to the next level with a brand new concept in retail sourcing allowing his clients to build their businesses even BIGGER and with more ease!

1. **Time Management**
2. **Sourcing profitable products**

Shawn has found a solution to both of those issues by creating his Retail Sourcing Team. He's hired a team of experienced professionals to scout brand new retail products, in original packaging, from established retailers that are guaranteed to sell! These deals enable clients to have a never ending supply of deals allow them to <u>save hours</u> of their own time searching for profitable deals while earning substantial profits on Amazon!

BOLOs posted Every Day
Our scouting team
*Searches in store daily !!*

The deals will be posted to the Private FB group that you will be given instant access to when you join today.

You will gain exclusive access to a spreadsheet of every deal we have ever found

You will gain access to an exclusive searchable app to use while sourcing in stores for Android or iOS

We provide on average 190 deals per month enabling you to have a wide variety to choose from to earn profits with

We share items under 100k rank and multiple sales per month. All of our deals will earn at least a 50% ROI

It doesn't get more committed than that and our smartphone app, alone, has received rave reviews making deal finding even easier! This exclusive app is state of the and allows you to sort by store, price, date or any other needed information for sourcing while in the store. Enabling you to leave the pen and paper at home! Our app includes links to the Amazon Page, Keepa, CamelCamelCamel and Price Zombie for each deal found. This is a great opportunity and space is limited, so scan here or follow this link to join now! http://retailsourcingteam.com

**Today You Are Being Handed the Guidance and Mentoring to Dramatically Grow Your Amazon Business to 6 Figures!!**

SHAWN MAYO'S
MASTER MINDS

Today is the Day When You Stop Guessing How You Are Going to Build Your Very Own Lucrative Amazon Business!

**We coach Amazon Sellers on how to effectively sell online and streamline their business processes! We help you down to business and technical basics, to sourcing and expanding your knowledge in the Amazon arena, as well as helping experienced sellers take their business to their next level and expand.**

- Limit of 50 members - private group (success without saturation)
- Weekly group coaching + weekly Webinar covering at least one new tool (Which business tool fits your needs?)
- Access to our Liquidation and Wholesale Sources
- Exclusive training by 6 figure Amazon experts in the Industry !!
- 200 BOLO's per month + over 40 archived training videos exclusive to members at all times with leading executives
- **Exclusive discounts with over 25 companies including:**

So, are you ready to finally have everything you need in order to take your Amazon business to 6 figures just like us? Scan or go here!
http://mastermind.shawnmayo.com/

## About Shawn Mayo

Shawn mayo is a coach and expert in out of the box sourcing techniques specializing in the grocery category with over a million dollars in total Amazon FBA sales. Shawn makes use of Facebook, Craigslist, liquidation for sourcing products. He also focuses on building relationships with couponers to source product for him and has built a large network of people who work with him sourcing his items. Shawn supports the community through his 3500 member Facebook group, Private mastermind groups, coaching and YouTube training videos.

## About Vallerie Wonders

Vallerie Wonders is Marketing expert with over 10 years of experience in her field. Combining a mix of professional leadership development and business strategy, Vallerie has quickly advanced in career working with national and global fortune 500 companies. She began her college internship working for the Walt Disney Company and continued by working with some of the country's leading executives at companies such as Pfizer, Merck, Novartis, and many more. Bringing innovative strategies and a humbled personality to the table, Vallerie has not only built partnering relationships with her clients, but more than anything helped them achieve their goals, build their teams and companies.